ATISHA
THE REVERED MONK SCHOLAR

Shashi Bala

GREAT INDIAN BUDDHIST MASTERS

wisdom tree

First published 2019

Photograph Credits: Christel Pilz, http://www.drukpavietnam.org, Creative Commons, www.drukpavietnam.org

ISBN 978-81-8328-476-9

Published by
Wisdom Tree
4779/23, Ansari Road
Darya Ganj, New Delhi-110 002
Ph.: 011-23247966/67/68
wisdomtreebooks@gmail.com

Printed in India

Contents

Editor's Note

In Buddhist tradition, the sun stands for wisdom (*prajna*) and the moon for the means (*upaya*) to achieve this wisdom. It is said that it was taught by one of the most profound proponents of Buddhism, Atisha, that these two should never be separated and that every human being has the capacity to achieve wisdom.

But who was Atisha? Named Dipankara-jnana, he was later given the honorific title Atisha, meaning the supremely genuine, incomparable one. Born in India in the tenth century AD, he became one of the greatest masters, responsible for spreading the knowledge and practice of Buddhism, not just in India but Indonesia and Tibet as well. To know about Atisha and the incredible life he lived makes his teachings more significant to those getting introduced to Buddhism—as is happening now across the world.

To bring back awareness, understanding and even the practice of Buddhism in the land of its birth, was the dream behind the idea of the series of books I dreamt of. To find the writers who would do them was not a simple task. There are today great practitioners and teachers of Buddhism but as the interest is spreading among people across the world, we felt it was needed to give a basic background and understanding not just about the philosophy but about those responsible for bringing Buddhism back into our understanding. And thanks to Shobit Arya and his Wisdom Tree publishing house, the dream turned into reality and the series was launched. Shashi Bala is herself a scholar and follower of Buddhism. She was the first person I thought of asking for doing the book on Atisha, after I saw the exhibition she had curated on this great Master.

Aruna Vasudev

ATISHA
THE REVERED MONK SCHOLAR

Atisha is the honorific title given to Shri Dipankara-jnana. Dipankara-jnana means 'one who has the knowledge of Dipankara, the Buddha of the past'. He lived in the tenth-eleventh century AD and was one of the greatest scholar monks in the history of Buddhism. He went from India to Tibet to work for the resurgence of Buddhism. He has been venerated by the Tibetans for around 1000 years but is almost forgotten by others. Over the past 100 years, scholars have begun to look into his life and the merits that he left behind not only for Tibet, but for all of mankind. His teachings did not favour any of the various Buddhist schools; rather, they were based on the essence of the philosophy that Lord Buddha preached to all who wanted to learn how to overcome suffering in this life. Atisha revived Tantrayana, Mahayana, Theravada and Vajrayana, and established what could be called Buddhayana.

We are not left with any written chronicles about Atisha from Indian historians. The major source that helps to study his life and legacy are Tibetan historical records collected over the past 100 years. They comprise biographies, doctrinal works, catalogues and hymns written in his praise.

A self-made image of Atisha dressed in a ceremonial way and enthroned in a shrine in a temple in Nyetang, Tibet.

left
Atisha's statue at the second floor of Shalu Monastery, Tibet.

Birth and Early Life

Atisha was born in 982 AD in Vajrayogini village, in the Vikramapura region of south-east Bengal, the present day Munshiganj district of Bangladesh. The royal city was a centre of Buddhist culture and academics. Atisha was the second among the three sons of Kalyanashri, a king of Sahor in Bengal, and his queen Shriprabha. The queen was revered like a goddess, a beautiful and chaste woman who worshipped the Triple Gem—the Buddha, the Dharma and the Sangha. Padmagarbha was Atisha's elder brother and Srigarbha, his younger brother.

When Atisha was born, as the biographies tell us, there were many auspicious signs. Flowers rained upon the city, a rainbow appeared in the sky and celestials sang hymns. The name he was given was also auspicious—Chandragarbha, which means 'womb of the moon'. In Buddhist tradition, the sun stands for wisdom (*prajna*), and the moon for the means (*upaya*) to achieve this wisdom. In all his later teachings, Atisha reminded his followers time and again to never separate the two, since every human being is given the means to achieve wisdom. But he warned that if people use the means in order to fulfil the desires of their senses, wisdom is unattainable. And they will not be able to follow the path to inner liberation. They will remain caught in the endless cycle of rebirth.

THE BIRTH OF ATISHA FROM DREPUNG MONASTERY

The biography of Atisha is painted on the walls of the room called 'Atisha's room' at Drepung Monastery, near Lhasa. It is situated behind the library of the Dalai Lama and connected by a corridor. There, one can see a picture of the palace, in which the queen is holding her new born baby in her arms, the king is sitting beside her and on the roof is Devi Tara. Devi Tara was Atisha's lifelong spiritual companion, giving him guidance and support whenever he needed them.

Atisha grew up in the Golden-bannered, a palace encircled by several bathing pools, magnificent gardens and forests of *tala* trees, surrounded by seven concentric walls, 363 connecting bridges, innumerable golden victory banners and thousands of noblemen. For the first eighteen months of his life, eight nurses in the royal palace of the capital city sheltered and attended on him. When he was eighteen months old, his parents took him to a local temple in Kamalapuri, where people from all over the kingdom had come to see the royal offspring for the first time. Atisha's potential as an extraordinary religious and spiritual leader could already be felt at that time.

Born with Rare Qualities

When Atisha saw all those people who had gathered there, he prayed that they may be possessed of merits like those of his parents, rule kingdoms that reached the summit of prosperity, be reborn as sons of kings, and be sustained by holy and virtuous deeds. He then proceeded to worship the holy objects inside and outside the temple.

Such a description of Atisha's first public appearance found in Buddhist texts and historical accounts portrays him as a child with the potential to become a great spiritual leader. On a visit to Vikramashila Monastery, he prostrated himself to the Buddha, the Dharma and the Sangha, and is known to have said, 'May I never be bound by worldly ways. May I be taught the holy way of the monks and humbly worship the Triple Gem. May I feel pity for all beings.'

Even though the prince was still young, he started to display a special capacity for learning astrology, the Sanskrit language, writing skills and the practice of the Dharma. At the age of six, he was able to distinguish between Buddhist and non-Buddhist doctrines. From then on up to the age of ten, he was happy to study all that was available to him, reciting prayers, obeying and serving his parents humbly and with sweet words, enjoying religious dances and sacred songs, paying his respects to holy men even from a distance, looking at worldly people with heartfelt pity and performing many noble deeds.

right
A memorial pavilion built by the People's Republic of China at Atisha Dipankara's birthplace following oriental architectural style in Vikaramapur in 2006.

page 11
A mural depicting the birth of Atisha from Drepung Monastery, Tibet, where Atisha can be see sitting in the lap of his mother below and on top of the roof he is receiving blessings from Devi Tara, his tutelary deity.

TARA
ATISHA'S TUTELARY DEITY

Understandably, Atisha's parents wanted him to be their successor as he was the brightest of their sons, but he was determined to enter the religious way of life. Yet, his parents tried their best to surround him with the luxuries and extravagances of royalty and even sought a bride for him. On the eve of his wedding, when Atisha was being taken in a procession of thirteen royal chariots beyond the great city, Goddess Tara appeared. She had been his tutelary deity many times before and continued to guide him in that life as well. She urged the prince not to care for power, and to be free from lust, as it would stain the *shila* robes he had worn before. She even reminded him that in all his previous 552 lives he had been an undefiled pandit. Therefore, as a holy monk he should seek his ordination in this life also; he should continue on the same path, seek the guidance of innumerable gurus and always practise the Dharma.

The ministers, parents and subjects did their utmost to please the prince but he just simply smiled. All that Goddess Tara had just said, he had known since birth. He explained to everyone around him that he needed to be true to his mission and thus, could not pursue life as a married man. After all he was born with super-knowledge that means seeing without eyes, hearing without ears and knowing the thoughts of others.

left
White Tara with seven eyes—three on the face including the forehead, two on the palms and two on the soles, also known as Saptalochani Tara, endows life eternal.

page 17
Green Tara at Kumbum Gyantse, Tibet.

GODDESS TARA

'Tara' comes from the root 'tar' in Sanskrit which means to save, to lead across. It means to cross over the ocean of existence, bhava sindhu. *She is the kinetic power of compassion (*karuna*) and saves (*tarayati*) the suffering beings; she is a saviour par excellence. She is popular as a merciful and benevolent comforter and helper of every soul in torment. She is invoked to save humans from the perils threatening mankind. She is naturally white in complexion, reminiscent of the brightness of the moon, smiling and graceful, looking like a sixteen-year-old maiden. She has seven eyes, is decked with all kinds of ornaments, holds her right hand in the* varada mudra, *the posture of charity, and a fully blossomed white lotus in her left hand.*

The Tibetan school of Tara begins with Atisha who laid emphasis on her cult. He also wrote a hymn to her. She became one of the most popular deities of Tibet after her two principal forms, white and green, were associated with the two wives of the great Tibetan emperor, Sron-btsan-sgam-po. According to a legend, the small gilt bronze statue of Tara, of Indian origin, placed at the altar of Samphu Monastery belonged to Atisha.

Meditation on the mandalas *of Tara and recitation of her sadhana texts begin early in the morning as a part of their daily ritual in most of the important Tibetan monasteries, praying for a long life, merits, wisdom and good health. When a devotee recites it, his body is filled with the nectar of immortality and white light begins to emanate from each pore of his body, forming an aura around him. The white radiance accomplishes the task of pacifying illnesses, evil spirits, negative karmic forces, mental obscurations and hindrances.*

Taranath, the great Tibetan master has transmitted to us several Indian tales celebrating her glories for the edification of devotees. Nagarjuna gives a detailed interpretation of Green Tara in his work in the Tanjur:

*'The goddess has a single face because the global knowledge of things is gnosis. The green colour points to the power of performing every kind of action. Her hands are two: the one on the right is the symbol of the relative or conventional truth, the one on the left is the symbol of the transcendent or absolute truth. Her right leg is stretched because the gnosis symbolised by Tara implies the renunciation of all kinds of sin. Her left leg is bent towards the body because this gnosis realises every kind of virtue. Her ornaments mean the perfection of knowledge and moral praxis. Her right hand is in the attitude of gifting in order to point out that the perfection of liberty (*dana paramita*) should be a companion of gnosis. Her left hand is in the attitude of protection because it protects creatures from all kinds of fear. She holds the lotus flower in order to show that from her all beings, taking refuge in her, derive their blessedness. She is conceived of as being sixteen-years old because she has the power to realise the welfare of all. She sits on a seat as white as the moon, because she is consubstantial with mystic knowledge.'*

On the Path of Enlightenment

One day, Atisha met a Buddhist hermit scholar named Jetari who reminded him of the ever-present Mara, the manifestation of temptations to deviate people from the path of purity. Kings, holy men and pandits are always the favourite targets of Mara, who wants to prevent the victory of righteousness and enlightenment. Even Siddhartha Gautama had to fight the challenges posed by Mara to thwart his attempt to achieve enlightenment.

Jetari advised Atisha to go to Nalanda, the leading Buddhist university in north-eastern India (in present day Bihar), to pursue further education. He told Atisha that in Nalanda, he would once again meet Bodhibhadra, who had been his guru in many of his earlier lives. There, he would also follow the footsteps of the foremost Buddhist scholars of the past, such as Shantarakshita and Kamalashila. Receiving lessons from Bodhibhadra would mean coming face-to-face with the Final Truth. Jetari urged Atisha to come back to him once he became a monk, promising to guide him further.

Atisha did as Jetari instructed. He renounced his kingdom, parted from his family and went to Nalanda. Bodhibhadra received his old friend in the then manifestation of Atisha with great honour, knowing in his heart who Atisha was and what his mission was going to be.

Bodhibhadra provided Atisha all the guidance he could and advised him to seek more teachings from another scholar, Vidyakokila, who was renowned for perfect meditation and his understanding of Emptiness, which the Buddha called Shunyata, the realm of enlightenment of the Formless. Vidyakokila furthered Atisha's insight into the path to truth and sent him to study more with Avadhutipa, a Vajrayana master, who was known to have attained the highest realisation. Avadhutipa did not want to teach Atisha immediately and sent him to Rahulagupta to first learn the Hevajra and Heruka Tantras and then to come back to him for in-depth studies on the secret mantra. Atisha stayed with Avadhutipa for several years, undergoing rigorous mental training and Tantra practices and rituals. Avadhutipa asked Atisha to consult Rahul-guhya-vajra, a yogi who lived near Rajgriha. When Atisha approached Rahul-guhya-vajra, he was given a test. The yogi threw a lightning bolt in his direction. Atisha just smiled, accepted it without fear and thanked the yogi for this special welcome. The yogi responded by introducing him into the Hevajra lineage, bestowing upon him the code name 'Indestructible Wisdom', adding to his knowledge by more expositions of Tantra and other precepts. What turned out to be one of the most important instructions Atisha received during these years was knowledge about the Middle Path, called the Madhyamaka way.

Atisha's teachers kept reminding him to always be aware that he really knew very little of all that was there to know. This was important even for a soul so spiritually advanced as Atisha. Humans usually tend to feel proud of what they learn and what they can do. Human nature is inclined to give in to temptations. Atisha resisted temptations, remained humble and continued to walk the path to enlightenment, and later, kept reminding his followers to do so too—to be aware of the power of the mind, to keep the mind free from desires and to always question when desires came up as to who was driving the mind.

Finally, the yogi teacher instructed Atisha to go back to his parents and ask for their formal permission to renounce royal responsibility. Atisha did as he was told, escorted by eight yogis and yoginis, determined to seek ordination.

When Atisha reached the palace and talked about his intentions, his parents at first thought he had gone mad under the influence of various teachers, but when he explained that he was doing nothing but following the mission he had been given at birth, his parents understood, remembering the signs that had accompanied the prince's birth, and they gave him their blessings.

According to Tibetan sources, at the age of about twenty, Atisha had mastered the philosophy of the three main Buddhist schools—Theravada, Mahayana and Vajrayana. But he never stopped learning. He wanted to understand all that was there to be understood about life. Further important insights he gained from his south Indian teacher, Rahulagupta of Krishna Giri, who initiated him into the esoteric (secret) system, thereby giving him the name 'Guhyajnanavajra', the one who has the knowledge of the secrets of life.

Atisha's studies were comprehensive and all encompassing. They included philosophy, logic, art, medicine, mathematics and engineering as well the non-Buddhist philosophies, including Vaishnava, Shaiva, Tantric Hinduism and other beliefs. After all, it was these philosophies with which Lord Buddha had been raised. Only after gaining enlightenment had Buddha taught what he had come to understand—the path everyone could follow in order to overcome suffering in this life and live in peace and harmony with all that exists. Atisha discovered that attaining Nirvana was not to separate oneself from the world, but to make use of the enlightenment to work with loving kindness and compassion for the benefit of all other beings.

Right since early childhood, Atisha had wanted to devote his life to the spiritual liberation of all beings, so he proceeded to accept the vows to become a Bodhisattva and requested to be ordained. He was formally declared a monk under the ordination by the great scholar monk, Shilarakshita, and given the new name of Shri Dipankara-jnana, meaning 'one who has the knowledge of Dipankara' or 'he whose deep awareness acts as a lamp' or 'one whose wisdom illuminates'. He could have hardly been given a more challenging name as this was the name of the first Buddha, called the Adibuddha, who lived long before Siddhartha Gautama. It is said that Dipankara was the invisible spiritual guide for Siddhartha to achieve enlightenment and become the historical Buddha, known as Buddha Shakyamuni.

After being ordained, Atisha travelled to all the holy places in India. Even though he had already attained a high status in the Buddhist community, he searched for more. He continued studying with the renowned Indian teacher, Dharmarakshita, who strictly followed the Buddha's instructions to keep wandering and spreading the teachings to people.

Altogether, Atisha learned from more than 100 teachers. Among them were Jnanashri, Krishnapada, Danashri, Ratnakashanti, Naropa and Prajnabhadra, all outstanding names in the history of Buddhism in India. It was one of the distinct characteristics of Atisha that he never showed any prejudice with any of them. He accepted all, though he later combined all his knowledge, cleared out what he felt was not in accordance with what the Buddha had said, and so revived what could be called Buddhayana, neither preaching Theravada or Mahayana nor Tantrayana or Vajrayana.

Atisha began to give discourses. Followers and students respected him so much that whatever he taught they could easily understand and adopt, even though he reminded them of the Buddha's warnings, to always evaluate a teaching before accepting it. Eventually, he was honoured with the title 'The Crown Ornament' of the Bhikshus, Bhikshunis and the lay community.

Developing Bodhichitta

One day, while on a pilgrimage to Bodhgaya, Atisha had a vision of two manifestations of Tara. He listened to what they said. One of them asked the other what was the most important practice to attain enlightenment. The other replied that one must learn to completely control one's mind so the mind becomes enlightened, which is called Bodhichitta.

Then on, inspired by the message, Atisha wanted to have a clear understanding of Bodhichitta and its practice. He fervently prayed to Goddess Tara, to be assured that true Bodhichitta dawns within his inner being. In one of the several visions he had of her, she told him that he should go to Suvarnadvipa to meet three important masters to receive their transmissions on how to be a true Bodhisattva and how to develop the Bodhichitta attitude. He prayed for blessings, and when the time was right, he knew he had to go to Suvarnadvipa, a place that comprises Indonesia today.

Shyama or Green Tara (eighth century) from Eastern India, Brooklyn Museum/Creative Commons

ATISHA
VOYAGES IN INDONESIA AND TIBET

Atisha was told by his Indian teachers as well that the best one to learn Bodhichitta from was a Buddhist scholar in Indonesia, called Dharmakirti, who is remembered by Tibetans by the name Serlingpa. At that time, the southern tip of the island of Sumatra, which was a part of Suvarnadvipa, was the main centre for Buddhist teachings. Buddhism in India had already started weakening following the arrival of Islam.

Dharmakirti was an offspring of the Shailendras, the royal family of Panangkaran. The question is: Who was Panangkaran? Panangkaran was the great wise man of Java who built a temple in honour of Devi Tara, called Chandi Kalasan, in the late eighth century. Even more important is that he was the conceptualiser of the unique structure of Borobudur in central Java.

Dharmakirti had come to India on a pilgrimage to Bodhgaya and had stayed there for seven years, learning under renowned gurus. His teachers were so impressed with his knowledge and learning capabilities, that they bestowed upon him the name 'Dharmakirti of Suvarnadvipa'. Dharmakirti means 'one who spreads the fame of Dharma' or 'one who became famous by Dharma'.

Voyage to Indonesia

Atisha was determined to find Dharmakirti. At the age of thirty or thirty-one, he took off

left
A mural from Drepung Monastery in Tibet depicting Atisha receiving the vase of wisdom from his teacher Dharmakirti in Indonesia.

for Indonesia. This seems to have been in the year 1011 or 1012. The biographies say that it took Atisha and his 125 companions twelve months of dangerous sea travel to arrive in south Sumatra. On the way, they had to face many tests in the form of violent waves, terrifying lightning, thunder and a huge leviathan that blocked their way. Sometimes, the danger was so threatening that they had to halt for several days, only to sail again when winds were favourable. All the while, Atisha kept praying to Tara for the safety of their trip and the success of his mission.

Finally, they arrived in the southern part of Sumatra and found the place of Dharmakirti's *vihara* at a village called Muara Jambi. They were received by Dharmakirti's disciples with great respect and honour. The disciples enquired about Atisha's life and studies and reported to their master that this Indian abbot was a great pandit, by the name of Shri Dipankara-jnana, who had come to study and understand the heart of Bodhichitta. Dharmakirti was overjoyed and asked the monks to bring him to his *vihara*. As one can read in the biography by Dromtonpa, who used to be Atisha's close companion in Tibet, Dharmakirti received Atisha with the words: 'The master of the Earth has arrived.'

Bodhichitta

Why was it that Atisha had to learn about Bodhichitta in Indonesia? Is Bodhichitta just one aspect or step on the path to enlightenment, just a door to be passed through in order to become a Bodhisattva? Or is it something more? It is said by Indonesian spiritual teachers that Bodhichitta is actually the soul of the Javanese people and the path from the world of desire and suffering to the realm of the true nature of all existence, where nothing obstructs anything, the realm of what Lord Buddha had described as Shunyata.

It means, Bodhichitta is not just one aspect or one step of the Inner Path, but refers to the deeply rooted and comprehensive philosophy of life of the Javanese people which goes back to days unknown. The essence of this philosophy is its link to the Almighty Creator, the One and only One, and to know, obey and realise the eternal and universal rules for living life in harmony. In order to do so, Javanese people train or even know from

page 26-27
Atisha with his teacher in Indonesia, Serlingpa and his chief disciple Dromtonpa, from Nyetang Monastery, Central Tibet, China.

the day they are born to control their mind, and therewith, the power of emotions. How can this be understood and realised? Dharmakirti told Atisha that if he wanted to really understand Bodhichitta, he would have to stay with him for twelve years. Atisha gratefully accepted.

Atisha's Stay in Indonesia

Dharmakirti arranged for Atisha to be introduced to all his monk and laymen community in a most joyful ceremony. Atisha reported about the difficulties they had experienced on the way there, but how they had never lost faith in achieving their goal. Dharmakirti asked how Atisha practised the rules of monkhood (*Vinaya*), realised the Buddhist precepts (*shila*) and showed impartial compassion for all beings. Dharmakirti was pleased with all the answers he got. Atisha stressed how important it is to keep the mind clean, to accept defeat and avoid bragging, to be moderate about everything and respect and serve others with ease. He also elaborated that one should never deceive oneself and never ever deceive God and the guru.

After Atisha and his companions were settled in their quarters, the great guru gave them a discourse on the perfection of wisdom (*Abhisamayalankara*) over fifteen sessions. In these sessions, Dharmakirti explained what needed to be understood about the law of dependent origination, which is based on recognition of the great teachers of yore, that all entities are non-arising, and as such, are uneternal. It was important to enable a teacher to properly explain the school of the Middle

DHARMAKIRTI

According to a Tibetan historical document by Bu-ston, from 1011 to 1023 AD, Atisha studied under Dharmakirti, who was the head of the Buddhist congregation in the isle of Suvarnadvipa during the reign of King Dharmapala. This means that Dharmakirti continued to live in Suvarnadvipa during the reign of the succeeding monarch Maravijayottungavarmadeva. The name Dharmapala does not appear among the names of the kings in Srivijaya annals. BR Chatterji, in his article entitled 'Jo Atisha in Serling and Tholing', has written based on the work of Prof G Coedes, a French scholar, that Dharmapala, the King of Suvarnadvipa, was also a teacher of Atisha. He has further referred to an early eleventh century manuscript with miniature paintings wherein the first miniature bears an explanatory note, 'Dipankara in Yavadvipa'.

Prof G Coedes has written that King Chudamanivarmadeva reigned in Srivijaya early in the eleventh century AD. It was during his reign that Acharya Dharmakirti composed a commentary on the text Abhisamayalankara. *In the sub-title of the Tibetan translation of this work, entitled* Durbodhaloka, *which is attributed to Atisha, it is stated that it was composed in the reign of Chudamanivarmadeva of Srivijayapura at Malayagiri (now known as Jambi, north of Palembang, the former capital of Srivijaya) in Suvarnadvipa.*

The only Indian scholar of our days to talk about Atisha, Dharmakirti and the concept of Shunyata is the late mystic, Osho. He said: 'First one has to become empty, not even clinging to emptiness; otherwise, life will never know the positive expression of religion. It will miss the poetry, the joy of sharing. Man lives in passion but when the mind disappears, passion is transformed into compassion. Passion means one is a beggar with a begging bowl, asking for more and more from everybody, exploiting others. When one lives in the mind, in passion, the whole of life is power politics. Even love, social service and humanitarian works are nothing but power politics. When the mind is dropped, the same energy becomes compassion and takes a totally new turn. The mind functions like darkness, and one is unaware of the light within. God is within, but because of the mind—mind means dreaming, desiring—one never looks within, goes on rushing outwards. The mind creates all kinds of misery. When it is gone, misery disappears, and suddenly one becomes full of energy that needs expression, sharing; it wants to become a song, a dance, a celebration. That is compassion.'

Osho further said: 'Atisha learnt from Dharmarakshita that there are two types of compassion. One is inactive compassion, where the meditator sits silently in his cave, showering his compassion over the whole of existence. He does not move or take any active step towards others; he will not seek and search for the people towards whom he can be compassionate. The other way of being compassionate is actively involving oneself, as was practised and shown by Atisha. He moved to Tibet to shower love on the Tibetans, transformed the Tibetan consciousness, acting as a miracle worker; Seven Points of Mind Training are the fundamental teachings that he gave to Tibet—a gift from Dharmakirti to Tibet.'

Way (Madhyamaka) to fully understand this. The essence of this school lies in its recognition that all phenomena are empty of inherent existence, and in its insistence that enlightenment is found somewhere between assertions of eternal realities and nothingness.

Thereafter, Dharmakirti told Atisha that he should go to Dharmarakshita, who lived in another cave nearby, as well as to Yogi Maitreya. This way he would get to know the ultimate reality, described as emptiness of misconceptions.

Dharmakirti instilled in Atisha techniques and practices to control the thinking mind. He explained that human beings are continuously tempted by passion and that their mind creates the ego, which creates illusions, and that leads to suffering. But when the mind is under control, passion is transformed into compassion. Dharmarakshita stressed on always being guided by love and compassion, while Yogi Maitreya taught the art of taking the suffering of others and absorbing it into one's own heart, known as love in action.

These important qualities were taught by the three Indonesian masters as the three ways for people to reach the realm of the Ultimate. Because Atisha studied under these three enlightened masters, he was honoured with the rare title, 'Atisha the Thrice Great'.

During his time in Indonesia, Atisha did not stay only in Sumatra. It was his ardent wish to visit the holy places in Java and elsewhere, which was somewhat like a homecoming for him. When he got to the home of Panangkaran on Boko hill above the Prambanan temple complex, it is said that he felt a strong sense of familiarity, as though old memories had come back to him. What must he have felt when his feet touched the sacred ground of such places as the Tara temple in Kalasan, when he walked the terraces of Borobudur, all built by Panangkaran? Tara had guided Panangkaran and now she was guiding Dipankara.

On the outside, Borobudur is such a universal textbook, where all about life on earth and the relationship between Creator and creation is explained in the architectural layout, in the structural concept of a stepped pyramid with nine terraces, topped by the Stupa of Shunyata, all resembling the ten stages to perfection of a Bodhisattva.

And the themes of the reliefs, the expressions of the carvings and the selection of the statues, their positioning in shrines and *stupa*s, the postures of their hands (mudras) are such that they speak the silent language that everyone can understand, that needs no translation. To study and understand this textbook takes time, patience, and most of all, on open heart.

It seems only natural that Dipankara spent quite some time at Borobudur. Was it to absorb its holy energy and eternal messages, some of which may still be stored like the *Terma*s in Tibet? Was it to refresh what he knew already? Was it to restructure his vast and diverse knowledge of the various Buddhist schools into one clean, clear and consistent line of teaching, herewith following Dharamakirti? Probably, all of these.

One must know, that Borobudur is not, as Javanese people will tell, a Buddhist *stupa*. Borobudur is the reflection of Javanese philosophy, but was built with Buddhist symbols and stories, because at that time, Buddhism was dominant in the realm of Suvarnadvipa, of which central Java was a part.

As Lord Buddha had explained the path to Shunyata in lessons and stories, it was easy to show this in the reliefs and easy for people to understand and follow. That means, that the teachings of Lord Buddha and the Javanese philosophy are basically the same, both are based on purifying the mind and overcoming the ego. What Borobudur reflects can be called Buddhayana—the original teachings before they split into several Buddhist schools.

Atisha remained on the island of Sumatra for twelve years as Dharmakirti had asked him to stay. During this time, he also had become aware that the basic lessons for everyone should be to train their mind and understand that there are various stages in order to reach the end of suffering, and that an essential condition is to understand and realise the lessons at each stage before one can move on to the next higher one. In Tibetan, this is called 'Lo Jong' (Mind training) and 'Lam Rim' (the stages of the path). Actually, all this had already been taught by Lord Buddha, Nagarjuna and others long before, but times had changed and there was a need to present the teachings in such a way that people could easily accept and follow.

Departure from Indonesia

Finally, in the year 1024, it was time for Atisha to return to India. There were several questions raised in connection with the reasons for Atisha to leave Indonesia at that time. Was it because the Indian Chola kings were attacking the Srivijaya empire or was it because Dipankara was needed in India? Was he called to mediate peace between the young King Nayapala of Magadha and King Karna, the belligerent neighbour to the other side of the river on the West—a story as told by spiritual gurus

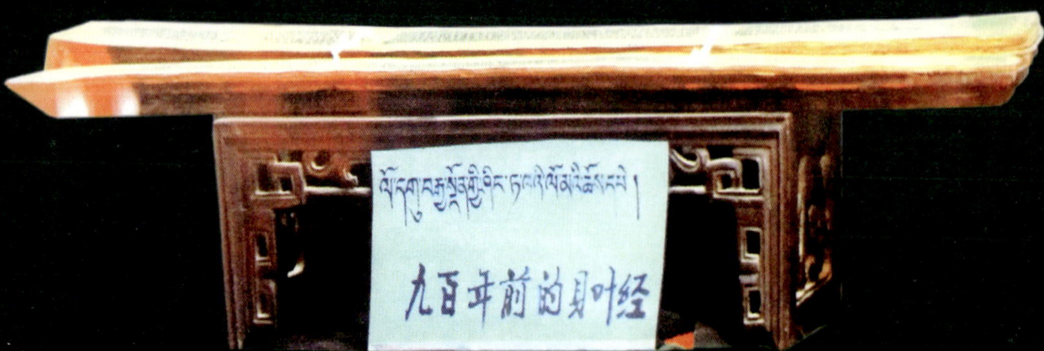

that sounds similar to how Prince Siddhartha, just before he left the palace, tried to prevent war between his father's kingdom and the neighbour because they quarrelled for water. As far as it is known, Dipankara helped to restore peace. Moreover, the influence of Buddhism there was deteriorating because of the advance of Islam. Was it Dipankara's task to collect and preserve the precious texts of former great scholar monks? Or had the time come to prepare for what seems to have been the greatest of his missions: to transfer the Javanese version of Buddhism to Tibet? All these questions are open for further research by monks and the academic community. Also, no one knows what had happened to Dharmakirti and the monasteries of Muara Jambi after Atisha left.

But before Atisha left, Dharmakirti composed six scripts which are considered the essence of Lord Buddha's teachings. They were not Dharmakirti's own thoughts, but commentaries on selected texts from great Buddhist scholars of former times such as Shantideva, Asanga, Nagarjuna and others. One would not need to study all those Sutras and Tantras, but could use these texts to open the door to the realm of the great treasure, taking them along wherever one goes.

SIX SCRIPTS COMPOSED BY DHARMAKIRTI FOR ATISHA

1. Abhisamayalankara-nama-prajna-paramita-upadesha-shastra-vrtti-duravabodha-loka-nama-tika *(TD 3794) is the magnum opus of Dharmakirti, a stupendous work on Mahayana philosophy, devoted mainly to a clear exposition of the highest* paramita, *namely* prajnaparamita. *It says in its colophon that it was written by Dharmakirti on the request of King Chudamanivarman, in Vijayanagar in Suvarndvipa. In Cordier's Catalogue, the author of the texts is mentioned as Acharya Dharmakirti of Suvarnadvipa and it is added that the work was composed during the reign of Deva-sri-varma-raja, the Chudamani, alias Chudamanimandapa, in Malayagiri in Vijayanagar of Suvarnadvipa.*

2. Bodhisattva-caryavatara-pindartha, *(TD 38 79, PT 5281)*

3. Bodhisattva-caryavatara-shattrimshat-pindhartha, *(TD 3878, PT 5282)*

4. Shiksa-samuccayabhisasamaya-nama *(TD 3942, PT 5338)*

5. Aryachala-sadhana-nama *(Otani Index 3883)*

6. Krodha-ganapati-sadhana, *(Otani Index 4994)*

Numbers 5 and 6 mentioned above are meant for tantric practices of two protectors. It may be assumed that the originals of these scripts still exist somewhere; they were written in Sanskrit or Old Javanese language. The originals may contain more than their translations in Tibetan.

left
A 900 year-old palm-leaf manuscript believed to have been brought by Atisha from Indonesia, is one of the precious relics preserved by the monks at the Labrang Monastery in Gansu province in China.

Back in India

After returning to India from Indonesia, Atisha, at the age of forty-four, stayed for about fifteen years in India and became even more famous as the foremost Buddhist scholar. He spent some time at the monastery of Mahabodhi, where he thrice defeated the Tirthika heretics in religious controversy, and thereby maintained the superiority of Buddhism over all other religions. He was later appointed as the head of Vikramashila Monastery at the request of King Nayapala. There was an intimate relation between Atisha and King Nayapala. On his way to Tibet, while in Nepal, he wrote a letter, *Vimala-ratna-lekha-nama*, to his dear friend, King Nayapala. This letter is still preserved in the Tibetan Tanjur, the collection of Buddhist texts.

According to Tibetan sources, Atisha's activities in India were centered in some of the major monasteries that had become prominent seats of learning. When he was appointed as head of Vikramashila Monastery, there were about 8,000 students studying under 108 professors, all of whom were eminent scholars. The courses included Therevada and Mahayana Buddhism, social sciences, Veda, Vedanta, Upanishad, philosophy, logic, medicine, science, astronomy, etc. Students from all over India as well as China, Tibet, Turkistan and other countries came to study here.

Though Atisha was the head of Vikramashila Buddhist University, he also held important responsibilities at Nalanda, Mahabodhi, Odantapuri and Somapuri monasteries. Following his activities, all of them came to prominence during the last phase of Buddhism in India.

According to Tibetan historian Sum-pa, Odantapuri was established on a hill in Bihar. It is further believed that the low mound near the station Bihar Sharif, on the way from Patna to Rajgir, was this famous Indian monastery, and the Tibetan monastery, Samye, was modelled after it.

The rise and fall of Somapuri corresponds to the rise and fall of Vikramashila, which was established in the eighth century AD by King Dharmapala of Bengal. Towards the end of the twelfth century AD, Nalanda and Vikramashila were desecrated, priests were killed and the sacred texts were incinerated by the Muhammadan conquest, leaving behind

right
Lord Buddha at Samye Monastery in Tibet where Atisha used to offer prayers.

only the spiritual teachings of teachers like Dipankara Atisha. Presumably, all the monasteries of eastern India, sponsored by the Palas and dependent on their patronage, faced a similar fate.

It was at Somapuri Monastery that two Tibetan translators—Viryasingha and Jayashila—worked under Atisha to prepare a Tibetan version of *Madhyamaka-ratna-pradipa-nama* written by the teacher, Bhavya, following the philosophy of Nagarjuna. Later, they translated it by revising it over and over again under the guidance of Atisha. It is also said that Atisha expounded Bhavya or Bhavaviveka's work *Tarka-jvala* at Somapuri. Its full title is *Madhyamaka-hridaya-vritti-tarka-jvala* and it is an enormous auto-commentary occupying about 5385 lines in the Peking edition of Tanjur. This account means that Viryasingha and Jayashila were together at Somapuri, and again met at the Vikaramashila university later, when Jayashila went there to officially invite Atisha to Tibet.

As the head of Vikramashila Monastery, Atisha's fame spread in all directions, and he received several invitations from Tibet to revive Buddhism which was then in a decaying condition. He earned fame as a debater, defeating non-Buddhists in debates on three occasions. When he came across what he perceived to be a misleading or deteriorating form of Buddhism, he would quickly and effectively implement reforms. The Mahayana and Tantric learning which had originated at Nalanda was subsequently developed and enriched at Vikramashila and spread to greater parts of Asia with the help of missionary activities by scholars.

State of Buddhism in Tibet

Buddhism in Tibet had almost been destroyed under the persecution by King Lang-dar-ma in the ninth century AD. Whatever was left was in utter confusion. The poor level of knowledge of surviving monks and laymen was often compensated by improvisation of actors-turned-self-styled gurus. Some Tibetans believed that ethical self-discipline and Tantras were mutually exclusive and that enlightenment could be achieved through intoxication and various forms of sexual misconduct. The doctrine was divided because most of the monks were no longer on the right path; those who followed Tantra turned away from Vinaya and those who followed Vinaya turned away from the Tantra. Tantras were destroyed. Some Tantrikas wrote them from memory which resulted in fragmentary texts. Others wrote some fanciful things. But they all claimed them to be true. Even some

ATISHA'S JOURNEY TO TIBET WAS CHALLENGING

Atisha was to go to Tibet. His guru, Dharmarakshita, in Sumatra, had predicted during his stay there that Buddhism in Tibet desperately needed rehabilitation. Going to Tibet was a challenge for Atisha as it is geographically very different from India. Goddess Tara had predicted that he may live for twenty years more if he stayed in India instead of going to Tibet which meant that he would cut short his life by twenty years by going there. Here, the sky is open and blue, land is pure, and peaks are icy, lofty and silent whereas the highest tableland, known as the roof of the world, is situated on a high altitude and served by the Himalayas as an effective barrier against rain clouds and for keeping the country dry. The land is poor and unproductive. The simplicity of the people there is combined with compassion and wisdom. Their life and thought is moulded accordingly.

The Tibetan source Pe-kar-cho-jung submits that there was no alphabet in Tibet before the time of Thonmi Sambhota or Nobel Bhota of the Thonmi tribe, a minister of Srong-tsen-gam-po. The name means straightforward, strict and profound. He came to be known so through his prowess and meritorious actions as a king who became an initiator of Buddhism and Buddhist literature into his vast domain by persuasion of his two wives—one was the daughter of the Chinese Emperor Tai-tsung and the other of the Nepalese King Ansuvarman.

Srong-tsen-gam-po commissioned his minister, Thonmi Sambhota, and sixteen other scholars to proceed to India to study the arts and sciences of both the Brahmanas and the Buddhists under the guidance of Deva-vit-simha in Magadha. According to his own account, he learnt the alphabet in Kashmir and gave the first alphabet to the Tibetan language, modelling it after the Indian Devanagari script. After returning to his country in 647 AD, he composed eight works on writing and grammar to initiate translation of Sanskrit texts into Tibetan. These were studied by the king himself for four years. Generally, two persons were engaged in translation projects—one master from India called Pandit and an adept interpreter from Tibet called Lo-tsa-ba. Jointly, they were known as Lo-pan. This way whatever was available in India in terms of religion and philosophy found its way to Tibet.

Great cultural activities coincided with the regime of King Thi-song-deu-tsen, in the second half of the eighth century. Translation works were undertaken in real earnest and on a larger scale. By the first half of the ninth century during the reign of King Ral-pa-chen, it reached its peak. Unfortunately, the king was assassinated, and all Buddhist activities came to a standstill during the reign of the next king, Lang-dar-ma, a rabid anti-Buddhist. The country sank into utter darkness. Again, by the second half of the tenth century, there appeared the great exponent of Buddhism, Rin-chen-bzang-po. From then onwards, translations continued without interruption upto the seventeenth century. According to the supplement attached to the Derge edition, the number of Indian scholars engaged in such projects was 107 and those from Tibet, 222.

of the so-called teachers from India went there and preached false doctrines in the name of Tantra. A full and correct understanding of the Dharma was far away.

The only place where Buddhism was still alive was the western Tibetan region of Nga-ris. This was thanks to King Yeshes-'od, who was a devout follower of Lord Buddha's teachings and had built many monasteries even though there were not many qualified monks anymore. But the ones who had survived and kept their faith had been travelling and collecting the remaining scriptures from all over the country while propagating the Dharma and keeping the torch burning. King Yeshes-'od was saddened by the distortions of the Buddhist teachings and the mixing of Buddhist practices with black magic. He made it his mission to revive the true teachings and therefore sponsored many Tibetan translators called *lo-tsa-bas* and Indian pandits, including those who were invited from India. The new generation of translators then started translating many Sanskrit texts to Tibetan.

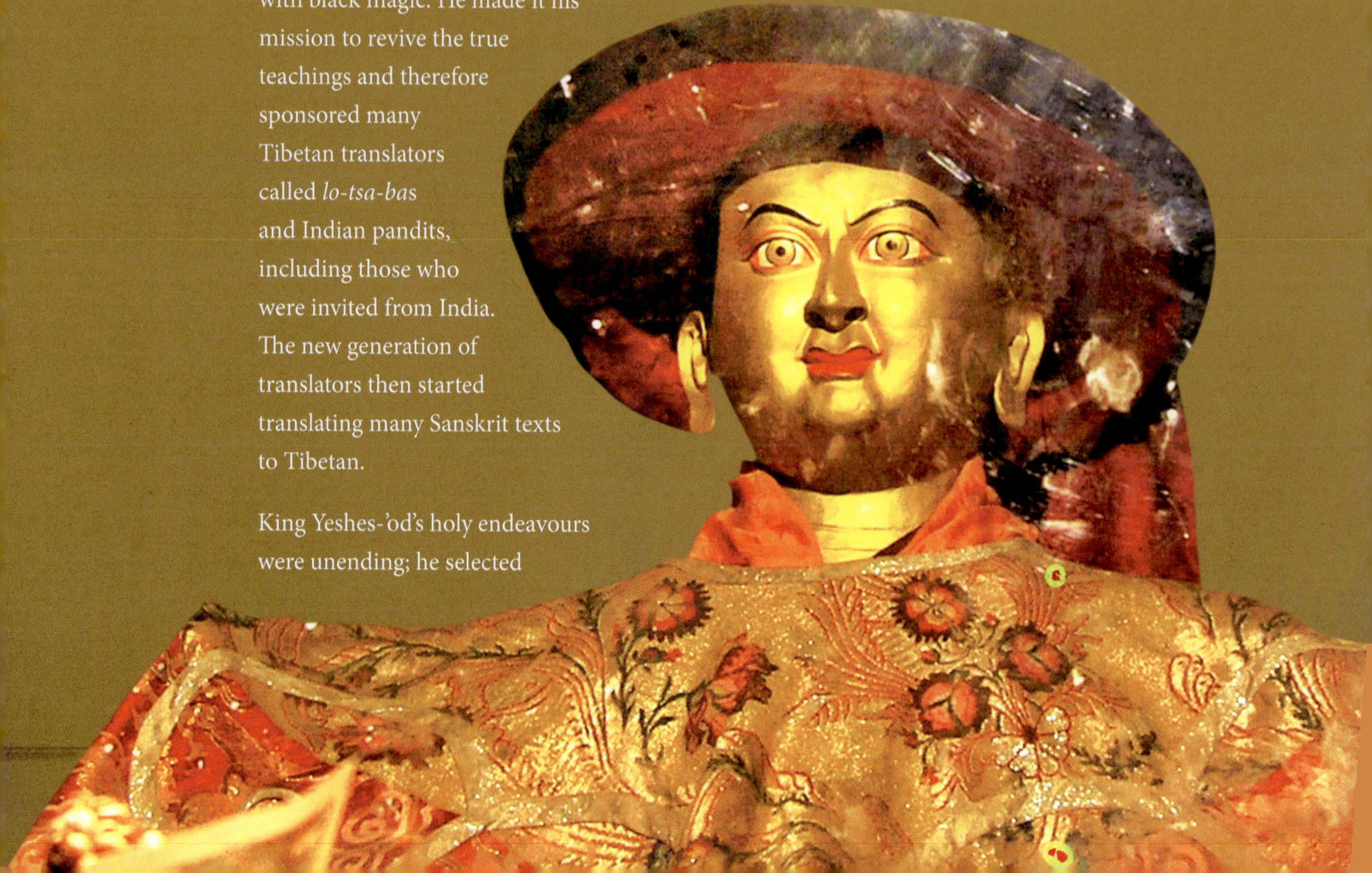

King Yeshes-'od's holy endeavours were unending; he selected twenty-one young men to go to India to study. Of this group, all except Rin-chen-bzang-po and Legs-pa'i-shes-rab died. Rin-chen-bzang-po became profoundly well-versed in all the branches of Tantra and philosophy. He translated many important texts and emerged as the greatest and the most respected Tibetan *lo-tsa-ba*. On returning to Tibet, these translators set the foundation for the revival of Buddhism; still, there was the need to bring a great pandit reformer to Tibet to explain and teach.

Plans to Invite Atisha to Tibet

Therefore, Yeshes-'od asked his monks whom he should invite and entrust with the mission to make Tibet a true Buddhist country again. Who would be such a well-versed pandit and where could he be found? Upon the advice of Rin-chen-bzang-po, Yeshes-'od decided that he should invite Atisha, and according to the customs of that time, he should present him with a large amount of gold as a sign of devotion. He sent his translators back to India to find Atisha. They tried their best to convince him to accept the king's invitation but Atisha felt that he could not leave behind his duties in India.

Sacrifice by King Yeshe-'od

King Yeshes-'od, however, did not give up. He collected much gold to once again invite Atisha. Meanwhile, the king of Garlog (Muhammadan king of Turkistan), who was against Buddhism, wanted to prevent Yeshes-'od from succeeding in his endeavour. He ordered his men to capture and imprison Yeshes-'od. Accordingly, the king was captured and put in prison. Hearing this news, Jangchub-'od, the king's nephew, went with a hundred horsemen to release his uncle, but the Garlog king put up powerful resistance. Jangchub-'od thought that since it would cost many lives, it would be unwise to wage war against him. Therefore, planning to get his uncle released by peaceful means, that is, by paying ransom, he approached the king of Garlog, who exclaimed: 'Either you give up your intention to invite the pandit and pay homage to me, or else you must bring me gold equivalent in weight to the body of Lha Lama (Yeshes-'od).' Then Jangchub-'od brought him a hundred gold coins as ransom, but the king refused to accept them. The next time, he took with him gold equivalent in weight to the body of his uncle, but again it was refused as it was less than the weight of his head.

left
Monk Lhalung is said to have hidden himself in a cave and meditated for twenty-two years, and his hat was kept there until 1959.

page 38
Atisha at Ganden Monastery, Tibet.

觉沃吉
PRECIOUS LORD

Then Jangchub-'od went up to the gate of the king's prison and cried: 'O compassionate one…I went to him with gold equivalent in weight to your body, but still he refused. I will come back to release you when I have collected gold equivalent in weight to your head as well. Until then, keep your mind fixed on karma, pray to the Triple Gem, and make merit by meditating on compassion.' On hearing this, his uncle smiled and said, 'I would have just ten years left. Therefore it would be better to die now for the religion. Do not give even one coin to the Garlog king. Take all the gold to India to invite Atisha and deliver this message to the pandit. He will spread Buddhism in Tibet. I shall pray for blessings to fall upon you in future lives. Now leave me here and devote yourself to the Dharma.'

Jangchub-'od was also worried over corrupt practices and the poor condition of Buddhism. He wanted to fulfil his uncle's dream and continued to persuade Atisha to come to Tibet. He sent royal messengers to Jayashila's residence at Tholing Monastery and asked him to go back to India. He told Jayashila, who had studied Sanskrit at Vikramashila College, that he must invite Atisha once again and tell him of the great sacrifice of the king. Jangchub-'od said to Jayashila, 'The holy doctrine of the Buddha has deteriorated. Messengers were sent twice to the great university of Vikramashila for inviting Shri Dipankara-jnana but with no result. Now you are accustomed to hot climate, you know the way to India and you can talk its language. So you should go as our envoy for the third time and bring the great Dipankara.'

Jayashila was also called Vinayadhara because of being well-versed in the Vinaya of Buddhist monasticism. Reluctantly, he said, 'Gracious King, I pray that this great command may not fall upon my small self. May I be permitted to carry on my studies for it does not lie within my competence to accomplish the commission.' The king continued: 'Jayashila, you should follow your sovereign's orders. The time, under any circumstances, whether you study or not, you shall have to serve the state and go to India.'

Invitation for Atisha

Jayashila set out for India. He was furnished with gold. A golden bar weighing sixteen ounces was given for being presented to the master while seven ounces were intended for himself, for expenses, and yet another five ounces for the interpreter. Gold attracted thieves and robbers, and Jayashila had several adventures on that account. Ultimately, he met a Nepalese prince and it was under his shelter and in his company that he reached the banks of the Ganga.

When Jayashila reached Vikramashila, he met Viryasingha from Tibet, who could easily recognise him as they had met earlier during their first visits to India. By then he had become a skilled translator from Sanskrit into Tibetan, and perhaps he was the earliest of the Tibetan translators who had worked directly under Atisha. Viryasingha was happy to meet him. Jayashila made a respectful present of a part of the gold that he had brought with him, and confided in him his mission.

On Viryasingha's advice, Jayashila became a resident pupil of Sthavira Ratnakara and begged him to introduce him to the holy saint master, Atisha. He observed: 'We Tibetans do not exert much influence, but still, I am well known to Atisha. He is fond of me. Tomorrow, there will a great assembly and 8000 *bhikshus* will congregate. In their midst, Atisha will come and you will gaze at him as a bright star, majestic and exalted.' When the next day dawned, Jayashila proceeded to the assembly. His record runs thus: 'At 8 o'clock in the morning, when the assembly congregated, I was given a seat in the rank of neophytes. The first to come was reverend Vidyakokila, noble, exalted and steady like the Sumeru Mountain. It is he who presided. I questioned those who were seated by my side if he were Atisha. But that was reverend guru, Vidyakokila, a lineal disciple of Acharya Chandrakirti, a saintly sage. He was the teacher of Atisha. My eyes roved and wandered, seeking out Atisha, and fell upon the Raja of Vikramashila who came and sat on a high seat, but none of the monks rose to honour him. He was followed by another master, grave and solemn, moving slowly. Young people rose to receive him with offerings of incense. The Raja also rose and the pandit was seated on a special seat. On enquiry, I was told that he was Vira-vajra, a stranger whose residence was not known to them. When all rows were filled, then entered Atisha, the venerable of venerables. Eyes gazing at his glory felt no satiety. His graceful and smiling face struck everyone in the assembly. From his waist hung a bundle of keys; Indians, Nepalese, Tibetans and everybody else looked at him as their own compatriot. Even the gods would own him as one of their kind. There was brilliance and simplicity on his face which acted as a magic spell and charmed everyone who directed his devoted eyes towards him.'

Another day, when Jayashila met Atisha, he explained: 'Next morning, I chanced to be at the place where the Acharya was distributing food to the poor. A boy who failed to get his share of alms ran after him and appealed: *Bhala ho O Natha Atisha! Bhata hona! Bhata hona! (Oh Lord Atisha! May you be blessed. May I get rice! May I get rice!)* On hearing the words "Natha Atisha", tears of joy flowed from my eyes. I followed him to his place and was about to tumble down from a bridge, my attention being wholly focussed upon Atisha. Atisha recognised me and my mission, for he said: "Ah Tibetan Ayushman (a way to address someone, meaning 'one who has a long life'), you are an honest people. Do not shed tears. I have much love for the Tibetan people, for your kings and ministers. You have come again for me without losing hope and patience. Offer your prayers to the Three Jewels, that is, to the Buddha, the Dharma and the Sangha."'

Jayashila further wrote, 'His words brought tears and hope into my heart. On another day I and Viryasingha went together to Atisha's place and offered the golden bar on a circular tray containing other offerings. These circular offerings were called *mandala*. Viryasingha described to Atisha, the spiritual thirst of the king of Tibet, and traced the history of the progress of Buddhism under the kings of Tibet as also the destruction caused by Lang-dar-ma, the apostate king, and finally, the debasement that then prevailed in the country. Viryasingha ended by appealing to cast a gracious look upon his benighted country. Atisha replied, "The king of Tibet is indeed a Bodhisattva and his three illustrious ancestors were indeed incarnate saints. I have a keen compassion for them. What personal sacrifices have they made for me, their wealth as well as their men; I love you Tibetans. But I am advancing in age and have the charge of the keys of my monasteries. A good many works remain unfinished. I cannot set out immediately. It is not a matter of personal feeling, of going or not going. Let me consult the deities and find out whether I shall be of service to your country and to the teachings of the Buddha." With these words, he returned the golden bar. Atisha had all the academic prestige but perhaps he was not the administrative head of the monastery.'

Atisha in a Dilemma

Then Atisha made many supplications to Goddess Tara, asking, 'Will it be worthwhile for me to go to Tibet?' Tara appeared to him and said, 'If you go to Tibet, the Dharma will be re-established in that country.' Atisha consulted again, 'If I wend my way to Tibet, shall I be of any service to the doctrine of the Buddha, shall I fulfil the wishes of the saintly king, and lastly, would there be any risk to my person and life?' The reply came: 'If you go, you will be of great service to them but your life would be shortened thereby.'

'Shortened by how much?' asked Atisha.

'By twenty years. If you remain in India, you will reach the age of ninety-two years. In Tibet, your life would last up to the seventy-second year only.'

Atisha was in a dilemma. Besides Vikramashila, a number of other big monasteries were being run under his guidance. Despite his preoccupations in India, his advanced age and the hazards of the journey, he accepted the invitation to visit Tibet for three years for the cause of the Dharma, and lay down this time-frame as a condition for his visit, so that he could return to Vikramashila. When Dipankara made his decision, Acharya Ratnakar Shanti, one of the senior Mahanayakas of Vikramashila said: 'India will be plunged into darkness without Dipankara. Keys to many Buddhist institutions are lying with him. During his absence, these institutions will be vacant. It seems that the shadow of darkness is around with Turkish soldiers seeking to invade India. I am feeling deeply concerned. Yet I bless Dipankara for his visit to Tibet in compassion and happiness for all beings.'

Atisha's Compassion for Tibetans

Atisha was moved by compassion for Tibetan people, by the accounts of ups and downs in the history of Buddhism in Tibet, the corrupt practices there and the story of Yeshes-'od sacrificing his life for the doctrine. He knew that the journey to Tibet at that age was going to adversely affect his health.

Atisha pondered, if my life would be shortened, I shall not mind. He subordinated longevity to

right
Atisha at Kumbum Gyantse, Tibet.

the good of the sentient beings. He thought that the Tibetan king had spent much gold for his sake and several people who came to invite him were smitten by fever. He felt sorry for them and called the two Tibetans and informed them of his decision. 'The deities have declared that my visit to Tibet will be for the good of Tibet, so I shall go. But you keep quiet. I shall not take up any new task, but will finish what I have in hand. It may take eighteen months. Till then, oh Ayushmans, will you wait?' The Tibetan translators replied: 'Not to speak of eighteen months, we would wait for three years. Only Your Holiness should consent to accompany us to Tibet.' They spent two years waiting for the master to be ready to leave.

According to some historians, Atisha pretended as if he was going for a pilgrimage to the eight sacred places of Buddhist sanctity, so that others may not know his intentions of leaving India. A monk who came to know of the intentions of Atisha, said to Jayashila that Atisha was like an eye for them, the Indians. In his absence, they would be blind. But he had no plans to stop them by any means; instead, he requested to bring him back after their mission was fulfilled.

Leaving Vikramashila

The departure of Atisha was painful for the residents of the University of Vikramashila. Sthavira Ratnakara told Jayashila, 'Do as I ordered you yesterday. Bring Atisha back after three years, and during this period accumulate all the wisdom that you can from him. Come back and complete your education with me. Atisha holds the keys to many institutions. In his absence, many monasteries will be empty. Evil signs loom large on the horizon. Turkish hordes are invading India, and I see evil days coming. Proceed to your country and may Atisha's work be for the good of all.' He further said to them, 'If Atisha comes back, then you accompany him. If he wishes to remain in Tibet, serve him there.'

On the way to Tibet, in 1040 AD, Shri Dipankara-jnana wanted to visit Vajrasana at Bodhgaya and other sacred places to pay homage to the Buddha. He was accompanied by Pandit Bumigarbha or Ksitigarbha, Bhumisangha, Viryachandra and a large retinue including Tibetans. They reached a small monastery, Mitra Vihar, on the Indian frontier. The monks at that monastery received them with veneration and joy. Bhumisangha has been described as Maharaja, the royal monk, the principle disciple of Atisha, the king of western India, majestic, bright and mighty.

After crossing the Indian frontiers, they visited sacred places of the Tirthikas (non-Buddhist heretics, especially Jain ones). Atisha's exposition to the Tirthikas was so impressive that a section tried to assassinate him by sending robbers his way. Upon entering Nepal, sometimes, he had to face extremely rude behaviour from the local chiefs. They even conspired a robbery but it was foiled by the master.

Journey to Tibet Via Nepal

Atisha spent a year in Nepal on his way to Tibet. His biographers do not give his exact route from India to Tibet. He must have taken the traditional route taken by traders and pilgrims through Champaran. The description of his journey to Swayambhunatha is full of glorification of his spiritual powers overcoming dangers and adverse situations.

An important halt was made at Swayambhunatha, the most sacred *stupa* of Nepal. The Raja of Swayambhu sent his officers to escort Atisha and his retinue from Krishong-bro. He made grand preparations for the reception and provided them large quantities of food and other necessities for their onward journey. Atisha conducted a religious service in the palace for the well-being of the king and the people.

Atisha presented an elephant as a gift to the king of Nepal, not for use in war but for carrying sacred objects, scriptures and images. From there, he wrote his famous letter to Nayapala, the king of Magadh, most probably at the time of his coronation. It is known as *Vimala-ratna-lekha-nama* and is considered to be a classic. The message contained therein was for the king to have compassion for all beings, to renounce evil in thoughts and deeds, to behave with humility, kindness and love towards all and to cultivate Bodhichitta. This was, in essence, a Buddhist message for peace and harmony within oneself and outside.

Atisha proceeded to a place called Holka of Palpa to meet one of his friends, a Buddhist sage who was deaf and who did not believe in the power of mantras. But according to Atisha, mantras and *paramita*s were both important to get enlightenment. He gave a complete discourse on *paramita*s for six days. He received a rousing reception from the king of Nepal, Anantakirti, when he was in Palpa. He wrote *Charya-sangraha-pradipa* on his request, which was translated into Tibetan by Jayashila. Atisha further urged the king to study the *sutra*s (Buddhist scriptures) in their entirety and listen to all the *shastra*s (commentaries on *sutra*s), guard the purity of his vow, keep his *shila* (conduct) pure, keep the openings of sense organs closed, practice yoga, beware of sins, meditate on the elements of the Dharma and perform Saptanga puja (seven-fold worship). He further advised him to meditate again if he failed to overcome disturbances caused by the imagination. He should observe the ten *carya*s (rules of conduct) prescribed by Maitreyanatha and offer his wealth to the Sangha and the helpless.

When Atisha's party was passing through Nepal, dwellers of plains and hill slopes offered

Tham Monastery in Nepal built by King Anantakirti inspired by Atisha during his stay on his way to Tibet.

QUOTES FROM CHARYA-SANGRAHA-PRADIPA

To the extent that one has kept
The vows pure and undefiled as explained
Pure in body, speech and mind, all three
Then one's conduct will be pure. (5)

With mindfulness, alertness, and deliberateness,
Ever guard the gates of the senses;
Night and day, three times each, again and again
Examine the (conscious) stream with your mind. (2)

Barring the doors of the senses,
One learns what moderation in food means too;
Persevere in Yoga, taking no rest
In the early and the latter parts of the night. (6)

Cultivate great sensitivity even to
The slightest defect [in yoga practice];
And dividing the night in three,
Rise from sleep in the last part. (7)

During meal times, say to yourself;
'It is by means of the essenceless body
That I must seek the true essence of things.'
We do not eat to become fat,
Nor do we eat for love of taste,
But to launch the mind's boat-like body. (11)

Between meditations, your conversation
Should be about the marvellous and the edifying;
And when you rise from sitting, walk a little
And circumambulate the stupa,
Reciting mantras or reading books, or
Even draw images of the Sugata. (13)

In general, when your mind is strong
In equipoise, do not emphasize
Virtuous activity of the body or speech.
But if your quipoise is not clear,
Then engage in all the good deeds you can
To make people well-disposed [to the truth]. (19)

Since this life, like a lamp in the wind,
Has little certainty of lasting,
One must begin in earnest to keep meditation
Like a flame burning in the head or body. (4)

What wise man is eaten up with doubts
About happiness in this life and the next?
It is for that very reason, intelligent men
Make meditation the essential thing. (6)

Though talking is fun, reflect on meaning.
The essence of the sugar cane is never in the husk.
The pleasant sought-after taste lies within.
It is impossible for a man to eat the husk
And get the sweet taste of the sugar cane.
So, talking is like the husk,
And understanding meaning is the taste. (44)

If the inner mind has been tamed,
The outer enemy cannot harm you.
When your inner mind is scattered, and
An outer enemy provides the occasion,

It is the inner enemy that inflames your (conscious) stream.
Therefore, you must conquer this inner enemy. (2)

Whoever has studied his own inner make-up,
Has (first) searched (how) his own mind (works).
Thus, when knowledge arises from its objects,
The objects are (perceived as) threefold:
Either afflicting, or virtuous, or neutral.
And depending on cause, circumstance and object,
The (resulting) Afflictions are of threefold degree.
Strong, moderate, or weak. (5)

Removing all hesitation,
Bend all effort toward perfection;
Do away with sleepiness and laziness,
And ever strive with perseverance. (1)

Proclaim your own sins, and
Do not search out the errors of others;
(Instead) proclaim the virtues of others,
And hide away your own virtues. (3)

Faith is the root of all religion.
And because this life does not last for long
Like a dewdrop on a blade of grass
The wise man does not become involved in sin,
Whose only result is evil destinies' suffering.
Practise the discipline of the Ten Virtues
And gradually, as far as possible, observe
Purely even the vows of Pratimoksha. (21)

In short, the Ten Religious Practices
That Maitreyanatha explained come down to;
The practice of a very attentive mind; and
Mindfulness that all is illusion. (15)

If you can afford it, contribute to the Community;
Or give a feast for ordinary folk;
For such giving to the unprotected
Increases the yogi's store of merit. (16)

When your day's activity is over,
And the early evening comes, compose yourself
In the True Nature—no mental activity at all;
Not even the activity of thinking. (17)

By the time midnight comes,
You will sleep the sleep of virtue;
Like the repose of the Lion [Buddha],
Whose mind is clear and rising. (18)

If one does meditation on Emptiness,
Neglecting correct Relative (Truth),
Then the world will deceive him on the other hand
In Relative thing like cause-effect, virtue-sin. (16)

Those who rely on little learning,
Unaware of vacuity of their knowledge,
And who make no effort to gain merit,
Such good-for-nothing persons are destroyed.
For when men of little insight are mistaken
In how they view Emptiness, they will perish. (17)

their respect. Atisha had chosen Viryasingha as his interpreter, but he fell sick. At the time of proceeding to Palpa, his illness took a serious turn and he breathed his last. And Atisha lost a faithful and talented Tibetan disciple. He was so distressed that he said, 'My going to Tibet, it appears, will not be of much value as my tongue has dropped off. I shall not be of any service to the Tibetans.' Jayashila tried to console the master by offering his services and by adding that there were many accomplished Sanskritists in Tibet who were eager to serve him. Atisha had no other alternative but to depend on him. He said, 'However, you are the best among the *lo-tsa-bas* (translators), I shall also be able to learn to speak Tibetan from you.' Jayashila had the longest association with Atisha and attended to him for nineteen years.

Atisha ordained Prince Padmaprabha as a monk pupil and advised the king to build the Tham Monastery, to which the latter agreed. Atisha left Nepal when the construction of the monastery began. After leaving Palpa, the party proceeded to Man-yul Gun-than.

From Nepal to Tholing

There is no documentation of which route Atisha took from Kathmandu to Tholing. The traditional route from Kathmandu to Mansarovar is via Muktinatha, Khochar Gumpha and Taklakot, that is Purang near Simbling. So it may be assumed that he travelled along this route. Some of the places along this route still keep Atisha in

THOLING MONASTERY

Tholing, meaning 'to fly without ever falling', is a tenth-century monastery founded by King Yeshes-'od. For many centuries, it remained the most important lamasery in western Tibet. Located on an escarpment above the Sutlej river, it was almost totally destroyed by the Red Guards. Wind and sand have eroded what was left. Some of the buildings at Tholing contain fifteenth- to seventeenth-century murals that are in fairly good condition. The paintings depict deities, high lamas and scenes from court life, showing foreign emissaries in Islamic, Chinese and central Asian clothing, paying respects to Tibetan royalty. Many of the paintings have been restored, preserving the ancient heritage.

After Atisha's arrival, the monastery became more reputed, and once again became a religious centre in Tibet under the royal patronage of the Guge kingdom. Although it faded after the collapse of the Guge kingdom, Tholing still maintains an important place in Tibet after almost 1000 years, in consideration of its significance in the second transmission of Buddhism into Tibet. Pre-1950 photographs of refined sculptures at Tholing witness the incredible devotion of the rulers of western Tibet.

right
A mural from Drepung Monastery portraying Atisha and his retinue being received in Tibet.

page 50-51
A view of the Tholing Monastery, Western Tibet, China. It was modelled after Samye Monastery and Atisha was given the first royal reception here by the then king of Tibet.

their heart. One of them, the Khochar Gumpha Monastery, is holy for the Tibetans because of its association with Atisha. It is believed that he had spent a rainy season there. While at this *gumpha*, he impressed the local people with his modest way of living, not depending on the necessities of life of a layman. Travelling further, he came to a place called Gejin. According to the Tibetans, footprints of Atisha can be found here. In fact, there is a place called Kangje, which literally means 'footprint'. Then there is a spring called Dup-chhu, 'the water of bliss'. Tibetans believe that this spring was dug by Atisha. Atisha's journey to Tibet across the mountainous terrain of the Himalayas amidst hazards makes for an exciting story. He reached western Tibet in 1042 AD. The Tibetans gave him a rousing reception on his entry into their country. Atisha was offered the first celestial drink, presented with a valuable tapestry inscribed with the image of Bodhisattva Avalokiteshvara.

Atisha's biography based on the personal communication of Jayashila gives a beautiful description of his travel towards Tholing, Golden Temple: 'Atisha surrounded by his companions…rode towards Tholing. The horse on which the great sage rode ambled gently like the walking of a golden swan. …His demeanour, personal beauty and his appearance, even at the age of sixty, made him worthy of divine honour. A smile was always present on his face and Sanskrit mantras were always on his lips. His voice was distinct, loud and impressive. His expressions were happy, oh, how sweetly he talked, and how noble he looked.'

Four generals with three hundred horsemen marched along the party, singing the welcome song. They proceeded to the monastery of Tholing. The King Lha-bla-ma, also known as Jangchub-'od, talked about the attainment of his cherished object. The senior general who escorted Atisha delivered a long welcome speech. A welcome hymn was recited by all those who had gathered to receive Atisha, conveying the meaning: 'O Great Teacher, you had such a long journey to Tibet through Nepal. It must have been extremely tiring. You are, of course, super human, so physical strain cannot be seen on your face. No fatigue can be traced in your eyes. It is so kind of you to visit Tibet.'

In his welcoming words, King Jangchub-'od said: 'You are the wisest and most meritorious saint. You have come from the land of *acharyas* (teachers) in the incarnation of a divinity in response to the

left
A group of Bodhisattvas at Sera Monastery, Tibet.

BODHI-PATHA-PRADIPA

Atisha composed the Bodhi-patha-pradipa *during his stay in Nga-ris at the Tholing Monastery of Guge at the request of Byanchub-'od. Byanchub-'od felt that there was a need for a solution to disagreements on several points of the doctrine among various scholars. Moreover, they needed a manual on Buddhism, specifically to serve the spiritual needs of the Tibetans of that time. There were outstanding students and scholars of Buddhist philosophy, but the theories and practices that were given religious sanction under the name of Tantra were annoying, such as drunkenness, debauchery and blood sacrifices.*

Atisha felt that the most important task at that time was moral reform without which philosophical wisdom would yield no result. According to him, prajna *without* upaya *and* upaya *without* prajna *was of no value. The* kushala *Dharmas like* dana paramita *are the* upayas. *One has to be a master of* upayas *to attain enlightenment. Practice of charity, morality, forgiveness, diligence and meditation are preconditions for philosophical wisdom. He explained the right systems of worship and meditation.*

Bodhi-patha-pradipa *illuminates the path for supreme enlightenment by prescribing the prerequisites—Bodhichitta, monastic rules (*vinaya*), Bodhisattva vows (compassion,* karuna*), super knowledge (*vipashyana*), calmness (*shamatha*), insight and means (*prajna *and* upaya*), higher vision (*prajnaparamita*) and the path of Tantras (*Tantrayana*). He explained that one should go to the refuge of Triple Gems (*trisharana*) if one aspires to attain Bodhichitta, with engaged intentions to work at liberating all sentient beings. According to Atisha there is no shortcut to awakening:*

Myself, I am not keen to reach, awakening in some swift way;
I shall remain until the final end, for the sake of but a single human creature.

Purity of body, speech and mind are essential to attain Buddhahood according to Atisha:

Purifying the actions of, my body and speech entirely;
I shall cleanse my mind's activity as well, no unvirtuous deed will ever be mine.

Although this is a comparatively small composition, containing sixty-eight verses, its impact on Tibetan Buddhism was stupendous. It contained the essence of both Sutras and Tantras. The fundamental theme of Bodhi-patha-pradipa *is universal emancipation, especially associated with the names of Nagarjuna and Chandrakirti. It is respected by the old and the new Kadampa sects.*

prayers of the people of Tibet. In this age, you are the representative of Lord Buddha and a paragon of Buddhism. All living beings and gods worship you for your purity.'

Stay at Tholing Monastery

During his stay at Tholing, Atisha delivered many sermons to the royal family, monks and the lay community. The most important text that he composed was under the title *Bodhi-patha-pradipa*, meaning 'the lamp to the path of enlightenment'. This sixty-eight-verse text became the mother text for the revival and reform of Buddhism in Tibet. Later, Atisha was asked to further explain it, and so he wrote an elaborate commentary.

A large number of important Buddhist texts were translated into Tibetan. The master gained wide popularity and acceptance, earning tremendous religious and academic prestige. He insisted on rigorous reforms, and when asked what is the highest teaching of the path, Atisha responded: 'The highest skill is in the realisation of egolessness. The highest nobility lies in subduing your own mind. The highest excellence is in having a mind which seeks to help others.' With such kind of teachings, the movement for Buddhist renaissance gained momentum. As a result, several members of the royal family lived their lives as monks without renouncing their responsibilities to the state.

Rin-chen-bzang-po and Atisha

The greatest of the Tibetan scholars of the time, Rin-chen-bzang-po's (Ratnabhadra's) submission to Atisha played a crucial role in Atisha's mission to reform and revive Buddhism. When Atisha arrived at Nga-ris, Rin-chen-bzang-po was in his eighty-fifth year and was well known for his knowledge of Buddhist teachings. At his invitation, Atisha went to his residence at Tholing Monastery, where Tantric deities were represented. The master composed laudatory verses for all of them. This amazed and overawed Rin-chen-bzang-po. The master thought that there was no

DROMTONPA: THE CHIEF DISCIPLE OF ATISHA

Legs-pa'i-shes-rab, a monk and Dromtonpa, an ordained layman and founder of the Bka' gdam-pa order, was the chief disciple of Atisha. The master from the Drom clan (1005-1064) met Atisha when the latter had completed his three-year stay in western Tibet and was planning to return to India but could not go back due to political disturbances in the border area. Dromtonpa sent messages to the scholars in central Tibet, requesting them to receive Atisha. He served as the foremost of his Tibetan disciples by organising many activities supporting the religious reforms.

勃伦敦巴
阿

need for him to come to Tibet when there were men like him. But he asked him a question: 'O great Lo-tsa-ba! When one is to practice *upaya* and *prajna*, how shall this be done?' The *lo-tsa-ba* replied: 'One should practice *upaya*, and then practice *prajna* separately.' The master exclaimed: '*Upaya* and *prajna* must always be practised together.' Rin-chen-bzang-po bowed to Atisha, accepting that he had been teaching it the wrong way. He realised that Atisha was the greatest among the great scholars. Atisha initiated him into *sadhana* (the method of appeasing a deity) and taught him the supreme importance of meditation to which he devoted the rest of his life. The great Tibetan scholar fully submitted to Atisha. He was famous as the greatest translator of his time, but he felt the need for his translations to be revised by Atisha and requested him to correct his translations of *Ashtasahasrika*, the *Vimshati-shloka* and the great commentary on the *Ashtasahasrika-prajnaparamita*. Then he translated a considerable number of works under Atisha's guidance.

After spending some years in Tibet, Atisha prepared to return to India as he had promised. The master along with his retinue journeyed as far as Kyi-ron, the town of western Tibet bordering on Nepal. But the road to Nepal was closed due to internal feuds. Atisha had no choice; he had to stay on in Tibet.

Travelling Extensively in Tibet

Atisha's principal disciple, Dromtonpa, urged him to travel and meet the many monks who were the guardians of Buddhist images, *stupa*s, shrines, sacred scriptures and relics all over Tibet. When Atisha agreed, Dromtonpa wrote to Kawa Sakya Wangchuk that all monks should welcome Atisha.

They did their best, honouring Atisha by wearing elegant shawls and their ceremonial garments which they used to usually wear on festive occasions as a mark of rank. They rode good horses covered with woollen blankets. On seeing them coming, Atisha cried: 'O Upasaka, who are these ghosts? Look at all those spirits approaching!' Dromtonpa told the monks that it would be more proper to be dressed in their *bhikshu* robes. They followed his advice, changed their robes, and then when they approached Atisha, he rose and returned their prostrations.

left
Atisha and his disciple Dromtonpa at Yunghokung Lamasery, Beijing.

When Atisha was on his way to Tsang, at Palpud Tan, he met Lhodrak Marpa Lotsawa. He regretted that they could meet only for a short time because Marpa wanted to visit India and Atisha was on his way to Sakya.

Pointing in the direction of Sakya, Atisha prophesied that an incarnation of Manjushri would appear there. At this place, Drokme Lotsawa bowed himself to the feet of Atisha as a disciple and venerated and served him meritoriously. He stayed in a nearby cave, praying and communicating with the monks. Later, a monastery was built on the holy ground called Sakya, the 'White Earth', towards the end of the thirteenth century. It became a treasure house of one of the biggest collections of sacred scripts in the Buddhist world. For centuries, a collection of manuscripts were hidden in the thick walls of the main prayer hall, and only a few years ago, these walls were opened and the scripts taken out to be preserved and read.

As Atisha was proceeding towards Narthan, he foretold that at that place an incarnation of Arya Sthivira would occur in the near future. Thereafter, he visited the shrine of Shalun Tel where he stayed in a rocky cave, and as usual, he preached many sermons, constantly reminding people to 'always study correctly what truly exists'. On leaving this place, he passed Buddhist Lent in Myantod, where he encountered three disciples—Yolchos, Yoldranron and Yoltag Bab. Disciple Golo also came and bowed at the feet of Atisha. Gonpapa, coming to the same place, did likewise, presenting offerings with the intention 'to strive for higher knowledge'.

Another important monastery in those days was located at Shalu, 22 km south of Shigatse. Atisha went there to pray and taught the people to pursue their spiritual upliftment. For centuries, Shalu Monastery remained a famous centre for scholarly learning and psychic training. Mural paintings at Shalu Monastery are still considered to be some of the most outstanding ones in Tibet. In the early fourteenth century, Shalu Monastery became the most important centre of learning under Buton Rinpoche (1290-1364), one of the great scholars of Tibet. It is the place where Buton brought together the 108 volumes of the fundamental

left
Yumbulakhang, the first palace built in Tibet by Nyentri Tsenpo probably in second century BC.

texts of Buddhism, the Kanjur and the 200 volumes of 'treatises and commentaries' compiled in the Tanjur. At the same time, he supervised the creation of 499 Tantric *mandalas*, a few of which still can be seen in the two chapels on the first floor. In 1305, Shalu was decorated by Tibetan and Nepalese artists who had been trained in Mongol imperial workshops under the famous Newari master, Arniko (1245-1306).

Atisha continued to travel onward to Yumbulakhang, the first palace in Tibet with a history of more than 2000 years. It is said that it was built for Nyentri Tsenpo, the king of Yumbulakhang who lived there in the second century BC. It is believed that this is the place where holy scripts fell from the sky around 1500 years ago. It became the summer palace of Srong-tsen-gam-po and Princess Wencheng. Later, it was converted into a monastery during the time of the fifth Dalai Lama. The towers resemble the defence towers in Tibet. The golden pinnacle is a later addition.

In the valley below, around the village of Mendro, Atisha was surprised to find 108 *stupas*. He built another one, called the Bungsha, which he devoted to the people. He kept teaching, staying there for three months. Later, the people of Mendro built a monastery to keep their memories of Atisha alive.

From Yumbulakhang, Atisha proceeded to Tangboche. There, the monks and the lay people wholeheartedly supported him in his great effort for the reform and revival of the Buddha's teachings, especially his teachings about the unity of practising insight (*prajna*) and means (*upaya*) together. He also kept reminding that conceptional thinking is of great ignorance. A short walk up the hill from the Tangboche Monastery is a small shrine, called Atisha Lhakhang, where Atisha liked to meditate. There, even today, one can see his carrying stick, one of the precious relics which was saved by the devotion of the monks.

From Tangboche, Atisha headed towards Samye, the first great Buddhist monastic university with a history of 1200 years, built by King Trisong Detsen, who was born and buried nearby. At Samye, Atisha was welcomed by Devaguru

right
The precious stick carried by Atisha that has been kept with veneration by the monks of Tangboche Monastery.

Bodhiraj and many other people; all of them wanted to listen to his teachings. To his surprise, Atisha found many Buddhist texts at Samye which he had never before seen in India. For Atisha, his visit to Samye had a very special meaning, reconnecting to the time when the first Indian scholar monks set foot in this place.

Sutras say that Insight divorced from Means is bondage and Means divorced of Insight is also bondage. Means is known as the collecting and Insight as accurately defining.

In other *sūtras* it is said that skill in Means is known as gathering up of all virtues and Insight is the skill of knowing that all phenomena are undifferentiated. The Mahayana *sutras* like *Mount Gaya* say that one truly progresses in the essence of *prajnaparamita*—perfection of insight and the other five *paramitas*—*dana*, *shila*, *kshanti*, *virya* and *dhyana* which are the Means. Insight delineates the Means accurately and effectively. When Insight analyses them correctly, only then they are effective; therefore when one adopts them for one's own and others' good, then absolutely no afflictions result. It is like a protecting mantra against poison.

Atisha belives that even a Bodhisattva must be grounded in both—Insight and Means and at all the ten levels of the Bodhisattva path he should continue practising them. The wisdom of an omniscient being rooted in Great Compassion and with the Enlightenment thought as its cause attains the perfection of Means.

According to Tibetan accounts, it was the Indian monk Shantarakshita, whose name means 'protector of peace', who found this site auspicious for building a monastery. However, all that was built kept collapsing. The workers were terrified. When Shantarakshita's contemporary, Padmasambhava arrived from northern India, he was asked to check what caused the construction to keep falling down. Padmasambhava then performed the Vajrakilaya dance and pacified the obstructive spirits so that the construction of the monastery could be completed. Thereafter, in 792, King Trisong

right
Dromtonpa, the chief disciple of Atisha at Ganden Monastery, Tibet.

page 64-65
The room where Atisha used to work and study at Drolma Lhakhang, Tibet.

种杰瓦
DOM-GYALWAY

Detson proclaimed Buddhism as the official religion of Tibet and initiated the ordination of the first Tibetan monks.

Samye Monastery was laid out in the shape of a giant *mandala*, with the main temple representing the legendary Mount Meru in the centre. Other buildings stand at the corners and cardinal points of the main temple, representing continents and other features of tantric Buddhist cosmology. As at that time, now again the main temple is full of murals and statues, many scripts and even relics.

Immediately after Trisong Detson had declared Buddhism as the official religion, he called Indian and Chinese monks to assemble for a great debate at Samye where the Indian scholars argued that the basis of Mahayana teachings was the assumption that it was necessary to accumulate vast quantities of knowledge and merit. The gradual process of enlightenment requiring good deeds and study was different from the Chinese teachings that believe in instantaneous realisation. What was to be accepted as the way for the Tibetans to be enlightened? The debate lasted for two years between the Chinese monk Hvashang and the Indian Kamalashila. Finally Kamalashila won the debate and the Indian system was established as the orthodox faith of Tibet. A great celebration proceeded and the emperor sang a beautiful song at the festival.

Then Atisha was invited by Khuton to come to Yarlun. But soon after, as Khuton did not behave well, Dromtonpa and others left with their master, embarking in a boat. Khuton, seeing this, ran after them and cried: 'Atisha, I beg you to stay.' But the master kept silent and threw his cap to him as a keepsake that would bring blessings. Atisha proceeded to stay at the shrine of Won at Keru for a month and drew a picture of himself on the wall there.

Finally, Atisha made his way to Lhasa. At that time, Lhasa was already the holy city for the Tibetans, as two of the holiest monasteries were built by the two wives of King Songtsen Gampo who was the founder of Lhasa. Being a Buddhist himself, he had married Princess Wencheng of the Chinese Tang dynasty and Princess Bhrikuti of Nepal. Both princesses brought sacred statues of the Buddha and other images as well as artists from their countries. Princess Wencheng is identified with the Jokhang and Princess Bhrikuti with Ramoche Monastery.

As everywhere else, Atisha was received with great honour and everyone wanted to listen to what this great guru had to tell them. Atisha reminded them to always guard one's own mind, not to cultivate friendship with an evil companion, not to be angry even if one gets harmed by another. Entering Jokhang Monastery, he was thrilled to look at the images of Avalokiteshvara and Buddha Shakyamuni. These did not look like mere statues to him; they were alive and could talk to those who approached them with devotion and an open heart. This is so even today. From Lhasa, Atisha travelled to many other places in the surrounding mountains, including Nyetang, Drak Yer-pa, Ganden and Reting.

At the time when Atisha went to the mountainside of Ganden, located 36 km from the Potala Palace in Lhasa, there was no monastery yet, but he predicted that one day this will be an important place for the dissemination of Buddhist teachings. Indeed, in 1409 AD, Ganden Monastery was founded by Tsong-kha-pa after he had a vision of Atisha. This vision inspired him to write the *Lamrim Chenmo*, the great treatise on the stages of monastery which became one of the most important seats of the Gelukpa school.

Another place where Atisha loved to spend time during summers were the rock caves at Drak Yer-pa, a mountainous area in the eastern surroundings of Lhasa. These caves were used already by King Songtsen Gampo and King Trisong Detsen in the seventh and eighth centuries. They were also the hideout for Lhalung Pelgyi Dorje after he assassinated the anti-Buddhist Emperor Lang-dar-ma in 842 AD.

Here, Atisha took residence in one of the caves and set up a small building on a hill, which served as a school. It is in ruins now, but at one time it had 300 monks, and for many years, functioned as the summer quarters for the Ramoche Monastery.

page 70-71
Samye Monastery, Central Tibet, China, where Atisha found many holy scripts which he had not seen elsewhere before. It was built by King Trisong Detsen as a symbol of the universe.

NYETANG
THE FINAL ABODE OF ATISHA

After having travelled for many years, without tiring of criss-crossing mountains and repeating his teachings hundreds of times, Atisha and his close companions—Dromtonpa, Jayashila as well as some followers decided to settle at a small temple at Nyetang, near Lhasa. Atisha wanted to have time to write, translate and leave behind as much as possible for all who would come after him. For meditation and worship, he used the small temple called Drolma Lhakhang, meaning 'the house of Tara'. The local people honoured Atisha by making him a throne out of mud and plants, which is still there, though it was recently covered by bronze plates for protection. Also, there is a statue of Atisha which he is said to have made himself. Then there are other relics, well protected in an enclosed space. In front of the temple are two small *stupa*s, one contains Atisha's personal belongings, the other contains relics of Dromtonpa who passed away ten years after Atisha.

Close to the temple, Atisha had built a house where he resided and worked. Moreover, he arranged for space to have two *stupas* to be set up, which resemble, on a small scale, the great monument of Borobudur in Indonesia. There he spent the last three years of his life until he finished his mission as Goddess Tara had instructed him.

left
A view of the rooms built near the cave at Drak Yer-pa, Tibet where Atisha used to work and teach.

Nirvana

When his end was near, Atisha passed on his worldly and spiritual knowledge, his experience and whatever else he could give to his disciples and the people around him. He also passed on his knowledge about healing and techniques for irrigation.

Atisha's disciple Dromtonpa (1005-1064 AD) urged his disciples to follow the master's wish to preserve his teachings by building monasteries for the monks at Ratoe, which is situated at an hour's uphill walk from Drolma Lhakhang at Nyetang. Some other monasteries built later to preserve and disseminate Atisha's teachings grew into big centres of Buddhist teaching.

The Legacy

After Atisha passed away in 1054 AD, Dromtonpa held the mourning ceremony and built the Tan-ma Hall near the Nyethang Monastery to enshrine a statue of Tara worshipped by Atisha as a Yidam (tutelary deity). As the last and chief disciple of Atisha, he was the successor of the Buddhist doctrines advocated by him. In 1056-57 AD, Dromtonpa was invited to preach doctrines in Reting/ Rwa-sgreng, where he founded a monastery. Taking Reting Monastery as the principal site for practice, he preached the doctrines taught by Atisha, laying the foundation for the Kadampa sect of Tibetan Buddhism. Thus, Atisha's teachings, especially the 'Rules for the Monks' (Vinaya) were preserved. Atisha had advised Dromtonpa that the Dharma depends on the Sangha and the Sangha depends on the Vinaya. The Kadampa school later evolved into the Gelukpa sect. An incarnate of Reting was regent to the eleventh Dalai Lama from 1847 to 1855, and then again for the twelfth Dalai Lama from 1856 to 1862 and another was regent to the fourteenth Dalai Lama.

Wherever Atisha had travelled and spent some time, even if it was only a single night, that became holy. At some places, he built monasteries while at others, his followers erected them in his memory. One such place is Drepung Monastery, where a room is dedicated to Atisha. His biography is painted on the walls of the room. Drepung Monastery was built as the foremost centre for Buddhist studies by Tsong-kha-pa's disciple, Jamayang Choeje, in 1416 AD.

right
Stupa from Ganden Monastery which is believed to have been carried by Atisha wherever he travelled.

Contributions of Atisha to Tibet

Until today, Atisha is revered as one of the most outstanding Buddhist scholar teachers preaching peace, compassion, humanism, self-sacrifice, harmony and amity. He was a keen student right since early childhood and never stopped learning. He kept reminding people of what Lord Buddha and many wise men before him had taught about life, and he carried the philosophy to Tibet. Atisha did his best to preserve Buddhist heritage in India, and later, in Tibet. He spent twelve years in Indonesia to study the practice of Bodhichitta in daily life. He accepted the invitation of the king of Tibet to come to the mountains and cleanse and revive Buddhism, which had been almost eliminated by King Lang-dar-ma in the ninth century AD. What was then left of Buddhism was distorted and corrupt, the doctrine was divided, monks were no longer sure of the right path, those who followed Tantra turned away from Vinaya and those who followed Vinaya turned away from Tantra. Monks no longer had the right gurus who, as Atisha had been saying so many times, were essential for giving the proper guidance. 'Without a guru for their eyes, they have not seen and will not see the true Mahayana path. Yet they preach as they please without a guru, satisfied they have seen the books.'

Atisha obeyed the advice of Goddess Tara to come to Tibet with the mission to re-establish Buddhism so as to prepare Tibet and its people to become the preservers of Buddhist heritage. The most urgent task for him at that time was moral reform, followed by philosophical wisdom. He urged the monks to curb their desires and not say that they are *bhikshus* just because they live in a monastery. He told them that they are no *bhikshus* as long as they harbour wordly desires and any thought of injuring others. Monks should always remember what they had promised to gods and gurus at the time of their vow, that they would not refuse even what is difficult to follow. He preached the necessity of the union of insight (*prajna*) and means (*upaya*), which includes the realisation of the six *paramitas*. These are charity, virtue, effort, patience and meditation, and when one realises these five, one can achieve the sixth, that is wisdom. Atisha referred to the *sutras* that say that bondage comes from insight being divorced from means, and means from insight as well.

left
Atisha, performing 'Turning the Wheel of Law' gesture, wearing the traditional 'pandita red hat' and attended by with his two main disciples, Dromtonpa on the right and Leg-pa'i-shes-rab on the left.

page 76-77
Drepung Monastery set up as the foremost centre for Buddhist studies by Tsong-kha-pa's disciple Jamayang Choeje in 1416.

According to Atisha, moral conduct is of foremost importance for a true Buddhist. He showed a progressive and clear structure to enlightenment by explaining the stepped path (Lam Rin) and the techniques of mind control (*lojong*). Over the years, Atisha managed to dispel the confusion in Tibet and reform Buddhism to bring forth its clear and clean teachings of what could be called Buddhayana. Atisha's teachings show us how to change our perspective in every moment of life, to transform our day-to-day experiences by accepting what comes our way without any anger or judgement. He urged monks and lay people to always have a smiling face and a loving mind, to always speak honestly and without anger, to be aware, and to avoid speaking senseless things so as to avoid making mistakes.

He never grew tired of reminding people that the door to the path of enlightenment opens with compassion and control of the mind, that one must cultivate the mind for spiritual development, accumulate merit and strive to achieve wisdom. Living what he taught, Atisha was an outstanding example for monks and the lay community. His examples inspired them to do as he did. The Tibetans loved him so much that they called him 'Precious Lord' or 'Jobo dorje pandit Atisha'.

Atisha wrote, translated and edited more than 200 texts, spread medical science, built reservoirs and translated many Sanskrit scriptures into Tibetan. He was even called the Second Buddha. By now, it is almost 1000 years after Atisha has physically departed from us, but what he left behind is timeless. He fulfilled his mission to ensure that Tibet's destiny became a treasure house of true spiritual knowledge. And by his doing so, the Tibetan people became the guardians of the eternal and universal rules of life, which are embedded in stone in the Stupa of Borobudur and which, 300 years after Atisha was gone, were somehow copied in a Tibetan version of the Kumbum Stupa in Gyantse.

Once again when the time was right, the Tibetan people fulfilled their mission to take these teachings all around the world and revive the great heritage of the ones who had acquired the super knowledge for the sake of all sentient beings. Atisha had gone from India to Indonesia, and later to Tibet, and in recent times, the Tibetans took their Buddhist heritage and planted it all over the world by opening Atisha meditation centres, not only in the East but also in the West.